CHICAGO
THEN & NOW

CHICAGO THEN & NOW

ELIZABETH McNULTY

THUNDER BAY
P·R·E·S·S

San Diego, California

Thunder Bay Press
An imprint of the Baker & Taylor Publishing Group
THUNDER BAY   10350 Barnes Canyon Road, San Diego, CA 92121
P·R·E·S·S   www.thunderbaybooks.com

Produced by Salamander Books,
an imprint of Anova Books Company Ltd.,
10 Southcombe Street, London W14 0RA, U.K.

All notations of errors or omissions should be addressed to
Thunder Bay Press, Editorial Department, at the above address.
All other correspondence (author inquiries, permissions) concerning
the content of this book should be addressed to Salamander Books,
10 Southcombe Street, London W14 0RA, U.K.

ISBN-13: 978-1-59223-732-6
ISBN-10: 1-59223-732-0

The Library of Congress has cataloged the original Thunder Bay edition
as follows:

McNulty, Elizabeth, 1971-
      Chicago then & now / Elizabeth P. McNulty
         p. cm.
      Includes index.
      ISBN 1-57145-278-8
         1. Chicago (Ill.)--Pictorial works. 2. Chicago (Ill.)--
      History--Pictorial works. I. Title: Chicago then and
      now. II. Title.

F548.37 .M37 2000
97.3'11--dc21
                                                        00-033792

Printed and bound in China

3 4 5 6 12 11 10

Acknowledgments:
Thanks to the staff of the Chicago Historical Society for all
their help negotiating the outstanding CHS photo collection.
Thanks to Carrie Urbanic for repeated hospitality, to Bobby Wong
for a thorough edit, to Martin Howard and Louise Daubeny at
PRC for all their hard work, and to Simon Clay for excellent
photos under difficult circumstances.

The publishers would like to thank Tom O'Gorman for his wealth
of updates in 2006.

Dedication:
For YDB, from Cassis to California, much love.

Picture credits:
The publisher wishes to thank the following for their kind permission
   to reproduce the photography for this book:

Images on pages 2, 7, 11, 13, 15, 27, 29, 31, 37, 39, 41 (both), 43, 45, 47, 49, 61, 63, 93, 95, 97,
   101, 103, 105 , 107, 111, 115, 119, 121, 123, 125, 127, 129, 131, 133 (inset), 137, 139, 141,
   143 (both), and the back flap image (bottom) courtesy of Simon Clay.
Images on pages 1, 6, 16, 18, 20, 24, 28, 30, 32, 36, 42, 44, 46 (main), 50, 52, 54, 56 (both), 58,
   60, 66, 68, 70, 72, 76, 80, 82, 88, 94, 96, 98, 100, 102, 104, 108, 110, 112, 118, 120 (inset),
   128, 130, 134, 136, 138, 140, 142, and the back flap image (top) courtesy of the Chicago
   Historical Society.
Images on pages 17, 19, 23, 25, 33, 35, 51, 55, 57, 59, 65, 67, 69, 73, 75, 77, 79, 81, 83, 85, 87, 89,
   91, 99, 103 (inset), 109, 113, 117, 133, 135 courtesy of Garry Chilluffo.
Image on page 8 courtesy of Chicago Aerial Surveying Company/Chicago Historical Society.
Images on pages 10, 12, 22, 34, 46 (inset), 74, 84 and 122 (both) courtesy of Barnes-
   Crosby/Chicago Historical Society.
Images on pages 26 and 92 courtesy of Kaufmann & Fabry/Chicago Historical Society.
Image on page 38 courtesy of Americo Grasso/Chicago Historical Society.
Image on page 40 courtesy of J. W. Taylor/Chicago Historical Society.
Image on page 48 courtesy of William T Barnum, from G1983.217/Chicago Historical Society.
Image on page 64 courtesy of Gordon Coster/Chicago Historical Society.
Image on page 78 (main) courtesy of S. L. Stein Publishing Company/Chicago Historical Society.
Image on page 78 (inset) courtesy of J. Carbutt/Chicago Historical Society.
Image on page 106 courtesy of C. R. Childs/Chicago Historical Society.
Images on pages 116, 124, 126 courtesy of Chicago Daily News/Chicago Historical Society.
Image on page 120 (main) courtesy of Essanay Film Studio Collection/Chicago Historical Society.
Image on page 132 courtesy of Richard Nickel/Chicago Historical Society.
Images on pages 9 and 71 appear courtesy of Corbis.
Image on page 62 appears courtesy of the Fourth Presbyterian Church. Special thanks to
   church archivist Bob Rasmussen and church administrator Mary Rhodes.

Pages 1 and 2: Wabash Avenue (see pages 12 and 13).

INTRODUCTION

It is hopeless for the occasional visitor to try to keep up with Chicago—she outgrows his prophecies faster than he can make them," wrote Mark Twain in 1883, when Chicago was just fifty years old. In that half-century, the city had grown to be the second largest in the nation, billing itself as "Boss City of the Universe." Not bad for a swampy parcel of land along a sludgy river, but then, Chicago's official civic motto is "I Will!"

The first Europeans to reach the area, Jesuit Jacques Marquette and fur trader Louis Joliet, arrived from the south in the fall of 1673. They paddled up the Mississippi into the Illinois and Des Plaines rivers, at which point they had to portage. They took a Native American trail, which led them to the south branch of the Chicago River, which in turn flowed northward into Lake Michigan. Joliet recognized the otherwise-dismal region's potential immediately: It would only be necessary to make a short canal to link the east-west Great Lakes system with that great north-south trade corridor, the Mississippi.

On a vast sweeping plain beside the "great water," the spongy area around the slow little river's mouth was called *che-cau-gou* by the Potawatomi Indians after the wild onion plants that grew there in abundance. The first permanent non–Native American resident of Chicago was Jean Baptiste Point du Sable, a black French fur trader, who built a cabin on the north bank of the river in about 1779. The region was incorporated as the "Town of Chicago" (population 300) in 1833.

With the development of the Illinois & Michigan canal in 1848, and the city's early simultaneous investment in railroads, Chicago became the leader in cattle, hog, lumber, and wheat industries, acting as a "golden funnel" to process and ship east the bounty of the prairie. Opportunities were plentiful, and by the mid-1850s, immigrants poured in at a rate of 100,000 a year. Chicago's secure location made it the Union's preeminent supply hub during the Civil War, and postwar Chicago seemed unstoppably prosperous.

Then, on October 8, 1871, the Great Chicago Fire raged through the town, laying waste to nearly four square miles of the city. With more than $200 million in damage and one-third the city's population homeless, Chicago's future lay in tatters, or so her detractors and rivals thought. "Chicago shall rise again!" crowed the local newspaper, and with "all gone but energy," Chicagoans went to work. Within two years, the entire city was rebuilt; within twelve, the city hosted 12 million guests at the World's Columbian Exposition, earning the nickname "The Windy City" for her boastfulness. The Great Fire united the citizenry as never before. By the late 1800s, Chicago had a population of over a million, placing her squarely behind a great city of the east. When a New Yorker deprecatingly referred to the "Second City," Chicago took up the moniker with pride.

The other positive to emerge from the Great Fire was the attraction of the nation's foremost architects. Chicago was wide open, a blank slate with no traditions but big ambitions. The resulting advances in skyscraper technology have led critics to hail Chicago as the "world capital of modern architecture." From the 1890s forward, Chicago's skyline sprouted a thicket of tall buildings, first masonry, then steel-framed, and is today home to three of the tallest buildings in the world. It was in Chicago that Louis Sullivan pioneered "functionalism," creating what is known today as the soaring Chicago School. Sullivan's student, Frank Lloyd Wright, revolutionized residential architecture. Instead of soaring, Wright's Prairie School designs take their inspiration from the horizontal planes of the Midwest and hug the earth.

Throughout, the "City of Big Shoulders" has had a reputation for toughness. "It is inhabited by savages," Rudyard Kipling wrote in 1889. Site of some of America's most notorious labor unrest (the Haymarket Affair, the Pullman Strike), Chicago became infamous for immigrant, and not to mention sanitation, abuse in Upton Sinclair's meat-packing exposé, *The Jungle*. Political corruption was rampant. In the twenties, Chicago was that "toddlin' town," a hangout for the nation's most nefarious crooks and gangsters (Dillinger, Moran, Capone). Then, with the post–World War II influx of African Americans, the city developed a reputation as among the most segregated of northern cities. Chicago is still fighting to right these wrongs, and signs—such as the election of the city's first black mayor in 1983—suggest the situation is improving.

Chicago today is a diverse and dynamic city, melding its status as international capital of commerce with down-home Midwestern good nature. Boston, Philadelphia, and New York owe big debts to European tradition, but Chicago, with her broad, spacious streets so perfectly rectilinear, and her gigantic, rule-breaking architecture, is 100 percent American. Chicago is America's immigrant city, a patchwork of neighborhoods creating a great American quilt. Home to the largest Polish population outside of Warsaw, Chicago also contains tight-knit communities of Mexican, Russian, Irish, Italian, Chinese, Vietnamese, Czech, Croatian, Lithuanian, Ukrainian, Armenian, Assyrian, and Indian immigrants—just to name a few. With a vast surfeit of attractions—the Art Institute, Field Museum, Shedd Aquarium, the Magnificent Mile, "duh" Bulls (Bears, Cubs), world-famous comedy (Second City), and world-famous theater (Steppenwolf, Goodman), not to forget the blues—"sweet home Chicago" is an American city second to none.

Chicago Then and Now pairs archival, black-and-white photos from the nineteenth and early twentieth century with full-color views from today to tell a story of the city's history. Historic photos may not exist for every street or neighborhood; likewise, historic streets or neighborhoods in a boomtown like Chicago may themselves no longer exist. Pairs have been selected based on symmetry (or lack of it), historic importance, and popular interest.

View toward the north-northeast, 1936. By the 1930s, Chicago was already taking shape as the home of America's boldest architecture. Some recently completed gems of the era include the thronelike Civic Opera Building (1929) at left along the south branch of the Chicago River; the hulking Merchandise Mart (1930) on the river's east branch, with 4.1 million square feet, still the world's largest commercial building; and, at center, Chicago's most famous Art Deco building, the Chicago Board of Trade (1930), topped with the pyramid.

Today, skyscrapers crowd the view—Chicago boasts ten of the hundred tallest buildings in the world. This view hovers over the Sears Tower (1974, 110 stories), the world's tallest building until 1996. The antennae seen here were replaced with taller models in 2000 to reclaim the tallest "height to tip of spire" title. At right stands Chicago's second tallest building, the sleekly rectilinear Amoco Building (1974, 82 stories), and at top right, the third of Chicago's big three, the 100-story John Hancock (1969).

Part of Daniel Burnham's grand Chicago Plan was realized downtown in the construction of Grant Park. Seen here in 1929, the new park was built on 220 acres of lakefront landfill in a formal French style designed by the Olmsted Brothers. At center is one of Chicago's most cherished landmarks, Buckingham Fountain. Modeled on the Bassin de Latone at Versailles, only twice the size, the pink marble fountain was installed in 1927. The Art Institute (1892) faces Michigan Avenue, whose skyscrapers dominate the skyline.

The prairie meets the lake along what Daniel Burnham called Chicago's "Emerald Necklace," the twenty-seven mile stretch of rolling lakeside parks. Nowhere is this seen more dramatically than in the explosion of public art in Grant Park (right), where soaring towers are joined to the shoreline of Lake Michigan. Millennium Park (left), the city's newest, is a 24.5-acre playland of wonder and elegance anchored by outstanding public art and architecture. Millennium Park boasts

Frank Gehry's Jay Pritzker Pavilion, a 120-foot-high open performance center of swirling titanium curls, with seating for seven thousand on its lawn; the Crown Fountain by Jaume Plensa; Anish Kapoor's *Cloud Gate*, a 110-ton seamless, elliptical, stainless-steel sculpture that reflects the city's skyline back upon itself; and the BP titanium pedestrian footbridge, also by Gehry, which snakes across Columbus Drive, joining Millennium Park to the Daley Bi-Centennial Park.

The nickname for downtown, the "Loop" refers to the rough circle of elevated rail (the "el"), completed in 1897, bounded by Wabash, Van Buren, Wells, and Lake streets, what Chicago novelist Nelson Algren called the city's "rusty iron heart." The el revolutionized turn-of-the-century commuting, with service to the south side, and later the west side, in almost half the time of streetcars.

El stations were typically built quickly with lightweight, inexpensive materials such as wood and sheet metal, but they proved durable. Although this station was later removed, several originals, such as the Quincy Street Station, are preserved today. The Rothschild Store with the ornate column in the archival photo has been replaced by another building (1912, Holabird & Roche), later Goldblatt's, and now owned by DePaul University.

This view north from Monroe Street, circa 1905, shows how the el bisected city streets horizontally and also vertically: the el was eye level with second-story windows. During an initial run in 1892 on what would become the Loop, one reporter noted that passengers witnessed "bits of domestic life usually hidden from the gaze of passing crowds." Although merchants initially resisted the el, they soon discovered that the trains brought hordes of people into the area as never before, and property values near the el skyrocketed.

Today, cars and pavement have replaced horsecarts and cobblestones, but Wabash has retained its commercial aspect. The three buildings preserved here, the Atwater (1877) and the Haskell and Barker buildings (1875), are considered the best examples of what the Loop looked like prior to the skyscraper boom of the 1890s. The white-painted iron facade of the Haskell was installed during alterations by Louis Sullivan in 1896. The old Silversmiths Building (1897) still stands, as does Mandel Brothers (1900) at the corner of Madison, where old Jewelers Row begins.

Left: State and Madison streets mark ground zero for Chicago's street numbering system, inaugurated in 1909. From this spot all addresses have their start. It has often been called "the busiest corner in the world." Louis Sullivan, Chicago's most inventive Prairie architect, set his masterpiece and last major commission, the Schlesinger & Meyer Department Store, here at 1 South State Street. Built using modular steel-frame construction between 1898–1899 and 1902–1904, Sullivan encrusted the exterior with his signature bronze filigree of swirling botanicals. Employing exaggerated renditions of the famed Chicago window, Sullivan created interior space bright with natural light. Along State Street, his windows quickly became showcases for merchandise to entice passing pedestrians. The store was soon sold to Carson Pirie Scott and became a mainstay of Chicago retailing. Two further expansions were undertaken with a 12-story addition by Daniel Burnham (1905–1906) and an 8-story southern addition by Holabird & Root (1960–1961).

Right: Carson Pirie Scott anchored State Street shopping for more than a century, enduring even through the economic decline of the street in the late 1970s and 1980s. While it remains one of the city's long-lasting examples of the Chicago School of Architecture, Carson's has recently announced that it will leave its fabled downtown location for good in early 2007. Plans are under way to introduce several retail stores to the area and reconfigure the building's interior for maximum use. Sullivan's masterpiece will lend itself to both upgrading and economic modernization, and will remain the reigning beauty of State Street, alive with the genius of Louis Sullivan.

For more than 150 years, no Chicago business was so closely identified with the character and glamour of Chicago life than Marshall Field and Company. For Chicagoans, Marshall Field invented the department store here on the prairie. He had one goal: "Give the lady what she wants." The enterprising retail magnate moved his business from its original location on Lake Street to State Street in the early 1860s, deepening the street's growth as a shopping hub. Even the Great Fire of 1871 could not keep Chicago's favorite department store down. Field's would eventually command the streetscape on State Street between Washington and Randolph Streets, occupying all of Wabash Avenue in a series of refined granite structures designed by Daniel Burnham between 1892 and 1907. Field's famous clock became a standard meeting place for Chicagoans.

Boasting an interior dome encrusted with mosaics by Louis Comfort Tiffany, the store featured more than 73 acres of merchandise in 450 departments. Sadly, the Loop's grandest enterprise ceased to be in September 2006. Having been purchased by the parent company of Macy's department store, the name and label of Marshall Field & Co. no longer exists. The black Macy's awnings have replaced the classic Field green, but the large bronze plaques with the store's original name can still be found on the four corners of the building—all that remains of the grand dame of State Street.

Until the 1860s, State Street was a cramped, muddy path lined with increasingly derelict balloon-frame shacks. Then successful retailer and would-be hotelier Potter Palmer invested in some land. Within a few years the street was widened and paved (with wooden blocks at least), and Marshall Field had taken up residence. By the 1890s, when this photo was taken, besides Field's and Carson's, there were several other major retailers—the Boston Store, Mandel Brothers, Siegel Cooper—each with an enormous flagship on State.

Chicago is enjoying an unheralded success in urban transition, in which former commercial buildings have been repurposed for domestic use. In addition, residential construction has transformed the character of what was once almost exclusively a commercial area of the city. Nothing demonstrates this more powerfully than Randolph Street, the very heart of commercial enterprise. East along Randolph Street from State Street to Lake Michigan, condominiums line the thoroughfare that borders Millennium Park and the lakefront. On State and Randolph Streets, Macy's department store—formerly Marshall Field's—anchors a square block with rapid change all around it. Rising along the west side of State Street is a square block of new retail and commercial space, including CBS television.

Left: In 1867, successful businessman Potter Palmer bought three-quarters of a mile of property on the ramshackle edge of town, State Street. Within two years, he had single-handedly transformed the area, convincing the city council to widen the street, inducing Marshall Field's to relocate from its premier Lake Street location, and replacing the tumbledown shacks at the corner of State and Monroe with the elegant Palmer House Hotel.

Above: The Palmer House seen at left is actually the second hotel. The original, which cost the then-outrageous sum of $300,000 to outfit, opened to great fanfare only thirteen days before the Great Fire of 1871. Potter Palmer rushed to rebuild, and in just a few years the rococo palace of the archival photo was completed. It was considered the grandest hotel of the day. Today, the Palmer House, a Hilton, is in its third incarnation, an elegant 1927 building by Holabird & Roche.

The "mother" of all glass and steel-frame skyscrapers—the Reliance Building by Daniel Burnham and John Wellborn Root—changed the course of architecture in the world when it was built in 1890. Located on the southwest corner of State and Washington streets, the remarkable use of large glass panes gave the world the classic "Chicago window," and the interior steel-frame construction introduced Chicagoans to modern design. Narrow piers, mullions, and spandrels are clad in cream-colored glazed terra-cotta, enhanced by a Gothic tracery and a flat cornice. Thanks to Mr. Otis and his elevator, there seemed no limits to the heights to which buildings could rise. Burnham, though, was devastated when his longtime partner Root died before the building was finished. In young Charles Atwood, Burnham found a talented genius with the ability to bring the project to completion. This photo shows the building circa 1900.

Despite decades of misuse and underappreciation alongside State Street's decline, the Reliance Building has been refurbished with painstaking skill and is now the Burnham Hotel. After a $27.5 million restoration in 1999, this architectural masterpiece once again shimmers with fresh elegance. In the interior, ornamental cast-iron framed elevators and stairways continue to showcase the genius of the building's great architects. This transformation brought back one of Chicago's most enduring historical landmarks, now named to honor the singular man who created it. One pane of original glass remains in place somewhere within the 14-story frame. The Burnham Hotel has also helped to jump-start a new prosperity along State Street. The hotel's Atwood Dining Room tips its hat to the young man responsible for completing this revolutionary addition to Chicago's influence on American architectural design.

Randolph Street east from Clark, 1910s. From the 1880s until the Eisenhower era, Randolph near State was Chicago's glittering theater district. The Olympic and the Garrick were two of the most important theaters. Housing the Garrick, the tall building with the delicate arches and cupola is the seventeen-story Schiller Building, designed by Adler & Sullivan in 1892. At the corner of Dearborn stands the rounded, Italianate-style Delaware Building. Down the block was the Roof Theater, located in the city's then-tallest building, the 21-story Masonic Temple (1892, Burnham & Root).

Today, Randolph is radically changed. In place of the Olympic, there is the Chicago Title & Trust Center (1992). The Schiller-Garrick was torn down in 1961 to make way for a parking structure, the Garrick Garage, which ironically incorporates some of the terra-cotta tiles from Adler & Sullivan's masterpiece. The Masonic Temple was demolished when the owners could not afford the property taxes—a fate not uncommon in Depression-era Chicago. The Delaware is now the Loop's oldest building, and the Oriental Theatre (1926) just beyond it is one of the last vestiges of the old neighborhood.

In the early 1920s, theater developers Balaban & Katz commissioned Rapp & Rapp to design two movie venues, the Tivoli (at 63rd and Cottage Grove, now demolished) and the palatial Chicago Theater. They would also later design another Chicago landmark—the Uptown Theater. The success of these models was so great that Rapp & Rapp went on to become "architects in residence" for the entire Paramount/Publix chain.

This Beaux Arts–style Classical Revival building was one of the first such buildings in the nation and is the oldest surviving in Chicago. The white terra-cotta triumphal arch behind the marquee opens into a series of lavish, Versailles-inspired spaces. The upright sign and marquee alone serve as an unofficial emblem of the city. The Chicago Theater was refurbished once for the 1933 World's Fair, but it would wait another fifty years before the rich Baroque interior was restored in 1986. Instead of movies, the theater now features live concerts and performances.

The First Methodist Episcopal Church, 77 West Washington. Built in 1923 and designed by skyscraper kings Holabird & Roche, the Chicago Temple is, in fact, a 21-story office tower, crowned by a soaring, neo-Gothic, eight-story steeple, the only church spire in the Loop. At street level, stained-glass windows depict church history.

Today, the Methodist Episcopal Church still occupies the ground-floor sanctuary and maintains a chapel in the spire. At 568 feet, the Chicago Temple ranks as the world's tallest church, according to the *Guinness Book of World Records*. Tall buildings now surround the church. From left: 33 North Dearborn (1967), 69 West Washington (1965), and Three First National Plaza (1981)—all three by Skidmore, Owings & Merrill.

Perhaps no single piece of Chicago architecture is more mourned or sadly missed than Louis Sullivan and Dankmar Alder's 1894 Chicago Stock Exchange, photographed here in 1928. Built at the corner of LaSalle and Washington streets, it was second in significance only to the New York Stock Exchange. Utilizing the technology of a caisson foundation to adapt to Chicago's marshy soil, Alder & Sullivan created an extraordinary design rich in detail. No other building in Chicago history was more of a cause célèbre than this when it was announced that it would fall to the wrecking ball in 1972. Its loss signifies a less intelligent era of Chicago architectural protection. No one worked more diligently to save the building than architectural photographer Richard Nickel, who, when the demolition began, managed to get inside to photograph the tragedy of its destruction. Sadly, Nickel himself became a casualty of the demolition—he was killed while inside the building. Later artifacts from the structure became treasured relics of the Prairie School of Design. The interior trading room, with Sullivan's gorgeous stenciling and stained glass, is preserved at the Art Institute of Chicago, as is the graceful entrance arch, called by one critic the "Wailing Wall of Chicago's preservation movement."

The Chicago Stock Exchange remained in the Sullivan and Adler–designed building only until shortly after Black Friday in 1929. By 1930, it had relocated. During the hardship of the Depression, the building remained vacant. Its subsequent history was a series of failed attempts to find someone capable of assuming the tax burden it posed. Today the corner of LaSalle and Washington Streets is void of architectural genius with the absence of the Chicago Stock Exchange building. In its place rises a structure of far more functional design, a monument to the era's blind eye to historical architecture and its legacy of true grandeur. Such important, irreplaceable architecture is more carefully protected today.

This Michigan Avenue streetscape (as seen from Randolph Street) in 1900 displays the revivalist Renaissance palazzo-style design of the Chicago Public Library, designed by the Boston architectural firm of Shepley, Rutan & Coolidge in 1897. This was the city's first purpose-built main public library. In the aftermath of the Great Fire of 1871, there was great sympathy for the unprecedented urban loss Chicagoans experienced. Queen Victoria, who was under the impression that a public library had been destroyed in the fire, joined writers in Britain and Ireland in sending full sets of their works to Chicago. In fact, no public library existed at the time of the fire, but Queen Victoria's donations offered a key incentive for finally establishing one. Over the next twenty-five years, a series of temporary locations housed a growing library system. On land owned by the Civil War's Grand Army of the Republic, the city was allowed to construct this grand edifice. Up the street is A. Montgomery Ward's catalog empire headquarters, built in 1899. From here Ward waged his long campaign to keep the parkland east of Michigan Avenue: "Forever open, clear and free."

With the relocation of the Main Chicago Public Library to the new Harold Washington Library at State and Congress in 1991, the fate of this extraordinary Chicago building was in jeopardy. It was saved from the wrecking ball by Mrs. Richard J. Daley, the widow of the longtime Democratic mayor and the mother of subsequent mayor Richard M. Daley. The soft-spoken Eleanor Guilfoyle Daley became the champion of this building. Through her intervention, an alternative municipal

use was found for this shimmering beauty. As the Chicago Cultural Center, it has been renewed as a space for art exhibitions, musical concerts, the city's Department of Cultural Affairs, and countless programs that connect visitors to the exhaustive opportunities for cultural experiences in Chicago. In the distance, the A. Montgomery Ward Building has become condominiums, minus its 10-story tower, which was removed in 1947.

The Art Institute of Chicago stands on Michigan Avenue at Adams Street. It was designed by the Boston firm of Shepley, Rutan & Coolidge as the Parliament of Religions Building for the World's Columbian Exposition of 1893. However, it stood outside the footprint of the main Jackson Park fair site. Unlike Daniel Burnham's temporary fair structures, this was built so it could be adapted for use by the growing Art Institute of Chicago, first incorporated in 1879.

Since the close of the fair, it has been home to Chicago's most extraordinary collection of art. A pair of bronze sentry lions designed by Edward Kemeys have guarded the entrance since 1894. At Christmas they are festooned with evergreen wreath collars. In 1986, when the Chicago Bears played in Super Bowl XX, the lions sported great Bears football helmets.

The Art Institute of Chicago houses the largest collection of French Impressionist paintings outside the Quay d'Orsay in Paris. This is due in no small part to the great generosity of Bertha Honore Palmer, the widow of hotelier Potter Palmer. In 1924 she bestowed fifty-two paintings, the core of one of the most remarkable collections in America. The following year, the Helen Birch Bartlett Memorial Collection was donated, containing *Sunday Afternoon on La Grande* *Jatte* (1884) by George Seurat, now one of the most visited works in the AIC's vast collection. Over the years, several additions have been made to the AIC, but today its most ambitious and defining expansion is underway—architect Renzo Piano's new building, the Modern Wing. When completed in 2009, the addition will have transformed the museum and the cityscape surrounding it, allowing it to flow into Millennium Park and altering the artistic flow of Michigan Avenue.

South Michigan Avenue circa 1890 featured several fine examples of the prevailing Romanesque style. The Auditorium Building stands at left, a theater-hotel-office complex that established Adler & Sullivan as pioneers of modern architecture. When completed in 1889, the Auditorium's eight-story tower on its south face, rising above the 10-story building, was the highest point in the city. At center, designed in 1885 with abundant windows to light carriage showrooms, the Studebaker Building was reborn in 1889 as the Fine Arts Building. At right, the original Burnham & Root–designed Art Institute.

Today, Roosevelt University occupies the Auditorium complex, having purchased it in 1946 and converted the hotel and office space into classrooms. The theater is still operational and famed for its superlative acoustics and sight lines. Home to the Chicago literary movement of the 1920s, the Fine Arts Building (*center*) today contains an art-film house on the first floor and numerous music and dance studios above. When the new Art Institute was built in the 1890s, the private Chicago Club purchased the old building at right; however, during renovations in 1929, the original structure collapsed. The new Chicago Club was inspired by its predecessor.

South LaSalle Street is to Chicago what Wall Street is to New York. Overlooking this canyon is the Art Deco Chicago Board of Trade Building (1930), designed by Holabird & Root with a pyramid roof topped by a thirty-foot statue of Ceres, the Roman goddess of grain. Founded in 1848, the Chicago Board of Trade originally promoted Chicago commerce in general, but changes in the grain market following the Civil War led to a new focus. By 1875, the city boasted a grain trade of $200 million and grain futures of $2 billion.

Today, the LaSalle Street canyon is refreshingly unchanged—at left, the Rookery and the Continental Bank, and at right, the Federal Reserve and the 208 S. LaSalle Building. The Board of Trade Building seen here is almost twice as large as the original, thanks to a dramatic 1980 addition to its southern face. The Chicago Board of Trade is today the oldest and largest futures exchange in the world, trading agricultural products as well as treasury notes, municipal bonds, and metals in its hectic, signature "open outcry" system.

After the Great Fire of 1871, a dilapidated structure on the corner of LaSalle and Adams housed a temporary City Hall. Whether named for the pigeons or the roosting politicians, the building became known as the Rookery. When Burnham & Root were contracted to design a new structure for the block, the name stuck. Completed in 1888, the Rookery, with its Romanesque arches, was considered "a thing of light" and "the most modern of office buildings."

Frank Lloyd Wright was not only the architect of the Rookery's 1905 renovation, he was also a building tenant. So too was Edward C. Waller, his greatest client and mentor, whose company managed the building. Wright refashioned the interior lobby atrium (*above*) using a style that can only be called a blend of Prairie and Persian. His signature modern style is apparent everywhere, partnered with a luxurious pastiche of Arabic refinements. This is Wright's only downtown Chicago contribution to architectural design, and his revisions were themselves restored in the early 1990s.

Dearborn Street at Van Buren, circa 1895. Designed by Holabird & Roche in 1894, the 17-story Old Colony Building was one of several Chicago School skyscrapers with gracefully rounded corner bays, designed to maximize desirable corner office space. Behind the Old Colony stands the Manhattan Building by William Le Baron Jenney. Upon completion in 1891, it was the first tall building to use skeleton construction throughout, the first 16-story building in the United States, and briefly the world's tallest building.

The Old Colony Building still carries the grandeur of
its nineteenth-century past, and with the remarkable
expansion of Chicago's downtown residential living,
the neighborhood has become a hot place to live. The
Manhattan Building by Jenney, the Plymouth Building
by Adler & Sullivan student Simeon B. Eisendrath, and
Burnham & Co.'s Fisher Building across Van Buren
Street make this a prestigous neighborhood of early
architectural innovation. Next door is the neo-Classical
Harold Washington Library, built in 1991. At 756,000
square feet and with 374,073 linear feet of shelving, this
is America's largest library and the second largest in the
world. Only the British Library is bigger. The iron
railings and tracks of the 1897 el fit the character of
the environs here, another remarkable expression of
Chicago engineering during the golden age of design.

View south from Adams Street, circa 1895. At right is the Monadnock "Building" (actually two buildings). Burnham & Root designed the northernmost building in 1891. A brick tower 66 feet wide, 200 feet long, and 200 feet high, the masonry-construction Monadnock has walls six feet thick at street level and was remarkable for its lack of exterior ornament. The southern addition by Holabird & Roche is a steel frame clad in terra-cotta. In the distance is the Dearborn Street Station.

Today, the block of Dearborn between Adams and Jackson is dominated by the Chicago Federal Center, actually an assortment of mid-twentieth-century curtain-wall buildings designed by reductivist ("less is more") pioneer Mies van der Rohe. In the midst of the plaza at right is Alexander Calder's vermilion-painted steel construction, *Flamingo*. The Monadnock Building, both masonry and steel-frame portions, still stands, as does Dearborn Street Station, although it is partially obscured now by the elevated rail.

Polk Street at the foot of South Dearborn, circa 1890. Designed by noted New York architect Cyrus Eidlitz in 1885, Dearborn Station (also known as Polk Street Station) caps the Dearborn Street vista. The brick Romanesque building featured a hipped roof complete with a Flemish clock tower. Toward the end of the nineteenth century, the station was among the city's busiest (*inset*).

The Old Dearborn Street Station has been the anchor of a vast revitalization in a neighborhood that was once crisscrossed with rail lines. The old station has been stretched beyond landmark status and has come back to life with restaurants, bars, boutiques, and several commercial art and cultural venues. Acres of new homes stretch for blocks, forming a new urban community created on the railroad right-of-way. Chicago's oldest passenger terminal has survived the upheavals of history, including a 1922 fire that destroyed its original, steep-roofed tower. Its replacement is a Renaissance tower that would be at home in Florence. Over thirty-five years after the closure of the station to rail services, Dearborn Station is as alive as ever.

525 South Dearborn, circa 1910. Designed by Baumann & Lotz in 1887, the original Franklin Building demonstrates how, in an effort to provide light for printers' detail work, architects began grouping windows by supporting them with cast-iron mullions. This gave rise in the 1890s to the "Chicago window," with its wide central pane flanked by narrow sash windows.

Once occupied by turn-of-the-century printing and publishing firms who built facilities near Dearborn Station, today Printers Row is undergoing a renaissance. The area's unusual street pattern of long narrow blocks provides maximum natural light, once a necessity for engraving and typesetting, now a delightful feature for loft apartments and luxury condos.

This retouched photo of an antebellum daguerreotype shows the Henry Clarke residence. When it was first constructed in 1836, this wooden Greek Revival mansion sat on a 35-acre strip of land that ran from near Michigan and 16th all the way to the lake. Owner Henry Brown Clarke, director of the Illinois State Bank, suffered severe losses in the U.S. financial Panic of 1837. He supplemented his income by farming and hunting wild game.

The Clarke House—Chicago's oldest home—has been repositioned twice. Its present location, 1855 South Indiana Avenue, is just several blocks west of its original site. Careful and historic exterior restoration has recently brought the house to life with soft colors and contrasting tones more accurately in keeping with its pedigree. During the process, the west portico was rebuilt, and shutters, moldings, and hardware that more faithfully fit the period of the house's construction were added.

The wooden house survived the Chicago Fire of 1871, escaping the pathway of the inferno thanks to the winds that sent the flames burning a northerly route from 12th Street. Clarke House remains a treasured piece of timeless Chicago real estate. The Chicago Architecture Foundation operates it as a museum. The City of Chicago recently established the Hillary Rodham Clinton Garden beside it, honoring the locally born former first lady.

After the Great Fire of 1871, Prairie Avenue, conveniently situated to the business district, became the neighborhood of choice for the city's elite. Home to the Fields, Armours, Palmers, Kimballs, Pullmans, Searses, and Glessners, Prairie Avenue was a showplace for some of the nation's foremost architects and featured houses of every period and style. The Romanesque Glessner House seen here is considered the foremost residential work of preeminent Boston architect Henry Hobson Richardson.

The industrialization and change that once pushed out Chicago's grandees from this stately Prairie Avenue neighborhood has come full circle. Fresh grandeur has returned, and Glessner House is once again surrounded by stately residences and restored mansions in one of Chicago's most sought-after new communities. Once again, a Prairie Avenue address is high end. The Arts and Crafts interior of Glessner House belies the simple architectural style inspired by H. H. Richardson's passion for Romanesque Revival. Under the auspices of the Chicago Architectural Foundation, the house is operated as a museum, allowing access to a treasured city building.

View north around the turn of the century. Chicago pioneered the rolling-lift (or "bascule") bridge, where the bridge splits evenly in half, with each weighted end functioning like a seesaw when released. By the time of this photo, the heavy river traffic and frequent bridge openings made north-south commuting a nightmare, stunting North Side development. Well into the twentieth century, industrial buildings lined the north bank of the East Branch.

Today, bridge openings are just as aggravating for drivers and pedestrians, although less frequent. What was, at the turn of the century, an industrial warehouse district north of the river is today a mix of upscale residential and office space. At left is the most famous example of Bertrand Goldberg's "organic" architecture, Marina City (1967), whose twin towers are known locally as the "corncob buildings." At right, with the bronze-tinted glass, is Mies van der Rohe's last American work, the IBM Building (1971). With the 2005 demolition of the *Chicago Sun-Times* headquarters—an aircraft carrier–styled low-rise glass-and-steel structure—the riverside now awaits Donald Trump's new Trump Tower by Skidmore, Owings & Merrill. At 1,131 feet, it is set to become Chicago's third-tallest building when completed, commanding an enormous chunk of the skyline.

From the early 1800s, the south bank of the Chicago River was the center of the wholesale produce market (*above*). The riverfront improvement project in the 1920s displaced the open-air produce and poultry market with the east-west segment of Wacker Drive, a decorative double-decked thoroughfare, seen here during the grand opening in 1926.

This section of Wacker Drive along the Chicago River (looking toward Michigan Avenue) was the site of the first official settlement here in 1803—the stockade fortress of Old Fort Dearborn. It was America's westernmost outpost at the time. Today the London Guarantee Trust (1923), the granite building at right, occupies the same land the fort once did. The shimmering white glaze of the Wrigley Building (1924) to the left, with its famous clock tower, sits on what was once the farm of Chicago's first settler, Jean Baptiste Pointe du Sable, in the late 1700s. The gothic tower of the Chicago *Tribune* (1925), across the street on Michigan Avenue, has the city's tallest flying buttresses.

Until 1920, Michigan Avenue stopped at the river. The north bank bordered on scruffy landfill; the roads were unpaved and lined with soap factories, breweries, and other industry. When this landmark "Chicago-style" bridge opened, it led the way for the development of humble Pine Street, the extension of Michigan north of the river.

It was the first double-decker bridge of its kind, accommodating cars up top and truck traffic on a lower level. By the time of this photo, a mere seven years later, the Wrigley Building was complete and the Tribune Tower under construction.

Today, North Michigan, with its unparalleled upscale shopping, is known around the world as the "Magnificent Mile" (so dubbed in 1947 by a real-estate developer). Crowding this scene are many newer buildings, such as the boxy Equitable (1965) and the neo-Deco NBC Tower (1989), but they don't really compete with the twin flights of fancy at center. Completed in 1924, the Wrigley, with its luminous white terra-cotta cladding, has been compared to London's Big Ben; it is brilliantly floodlit at night. At right, the Tribune Tower's design resulted from a 1922 competition to create "the most beautiful office building in the world." Howells & Hood's Gothic structure, complete with flying buttresses, was built in 1925 and is inset with stones from famous monuments around the world such as the Parthenon, Notre Dame, and the Pyramids.

Photo circa 1891. It wasn't until the 1860s that the "city on the lake" obtained good-quality drinking water. Chicagoans were accustomed to foul, muddy, even fishy water until the construction of the waterworks in 1866, which drew water from two miles out. To provide water pressure, a standpipe was constructed; the 154-foot tower housing it was designed by William Boyington in Joliet limestone in a style that has been called "naive Gothic." On a visit to the city, Oscar Wilde called it something else: "A castellated monstrosity with pepper boxes stuck all over it."

Today, the Chicago Water Tower is one of the city's best-loved monuments. One of only a handful of structures to survive the Great Fire of 1871, it became a symbol of the city's will to survive. The tower has been obsolete since 1906, but it is meticulously preserved and spotlit at night. The pumping station contains the city's tourist information center. The tallest building on north Michigan until 1920, the Water Tower today is dwarfed by one of Chicago's tallest (and most famous) buildings, the 100-story John Hancock, completed in 1969. Water Tower Place (1976) is at right.

The founders of this congregation inaugurated their first church on October 8, 1871, just hours before the Great Fire raged through the city. The first structure was burned to the ground, and all but five church members lost their homes. In February 1874, the congregation dedicated a new facility on the northwest corner of Rush and Superior streets. After forty years at this location, the growing congregation and its many programs called for a new facility. The wealthy congregation hired famed Boston architect Ralph Adams Cram.

Cram's impressive Gothic Revival church building at the corner of Michigan and Chestnut opened in 1914 after two years of construction. The location was a gamble, as Chicago's now famous "Magnificent Mile" was then just an underdeveloped road called Pine Street. It wasn't until the construction of the Michigan Avenue Bridge in 1920 that North Michigan took off. Today, except for the familiar Water Tower two blocks to the south, Fourth Church is the oldest surviving structure on Michigan Avenue north of the river.

View looking east toward the Drake Hotel. Until the 1920 construction of the Michigan Avenue Bridge, with its double decks of traffic, the frequent openings of the other bascule bridges made the north side of the river difficult to access, and development was slow. North Michigan was known as "Pine Street," home to a variety of industrial factories. Oak Street, seen here in the 1930s, was a lower-rent residential district. In the distance, the tall structure on the right is the splendid Art Deco Palmolive Building with rotating Lindberg Beacon on Michigan Avenue. At the time of this photo in the early 1930s, it was the single tallest structure in the neighborhood. The tall building under construction in the distance (center), the Drake Towers, is one of the East Lake Shore Drive towers that marks out the elegant residential buildings along the posh lakefront of Oak Street Beach.

The view looking east toward North Michigan Avenue today has been dramatically altered. High-rise dwellings crowd the skyline, and the rough neighborhood of yesteryear is now tight with expensive low-rise condos. A totally new and leafy extension of the "Gold Coast" community has replaced the run-down rooming houses and corner taverns. Farther east, between Rush Street and Michigan Avenue, Oak Street morphs into the city's most exclusive fashion venue. World-famous jewelers and couture boutiques stand shoulder-to-shoulder alongside Barneys New York, creating a paradise for shoppers.

Lake Shore Drive is so much a part of Chicago's identity that it is difficult to imagine a time it did not exist. Nevertheless, Michigan Avenue constituted the easternmost street for downtown's lakefront until several changes in shoreline, namely, the filling of the Grant Park area and Streeterville in the later 1800s. By the time of this photo (1914, view south from Oak), Daniel Burnham's great Plan of Chicago (1906) had set aside the lakefront for the enjoyment of all citizens, and Lake Shore Drive connected all twenty-nine miles of it.

Today, Lake Shore Drive is fully developed and provides some of the most gorgeous views of the city. In 1884, successful businessman Potter Palmer built an elaborate mansion on the otherwise desolate lakefront, giving an impetus to construction along what would become the drive. Just twenty years later, one commentator wrote, "Along Lake Shore Drive you will find the homes of all the great merchants, the makers of Chicago." Much of Lake Shore Drive, particularly north of the city, is still lined with luxury apartment buildings.

View south, 1922. With the residential boom on the newly created Lake Shore Drive (note the high-rise apartment buildings) came the demand for beaches. The city's first public facility, the Lincoln Park Beach, opened in 1895, and because "bathing" was still a new sport, the first swimmer went au naturel. By 1916, the city had three beaches and four inland pools with a combined attendance of 1.2 million people.

Today, the white sandy strip off Oak Street is Chicago's most fashionable beach, the place for beautiful people to sunbathe, see and be seen, and even sometimes swim. A natural beach, Oak Street still requires imported sand from time to time, due to wintertime erosion by the choppy waters of Lake Michigan. Luxury residential buildings have continued to sprout on Lake Shore Drive, and this beach provides a lovely view of the downtown skyline.

Municipal Pier No. 2 was the only pier built by the city out of a plan for five piers. Constructed in 1916, the pier, at 3,000 feet in length, was then the world's longest. During the 1920s, when this photo was taken, the pier served both commercial and excursion vessels, seen here lined up as throngs of people crowd the dock. The U.S. Navy occupied the pier during World War II (thus the name), and later the pier became the original Chicago campus of the University of Illinois.

After decades of stagnation, Navy Pier has been brought back to life as one of Chicago's most sought after destinations. A dramatic process of restoration began in 1976 and only ended in 1994. When completed, the pier was a 525-acre playground that included the Grand Ballroom, a 138-foot-by-150-foot hall with a 100-foot-high half-domed ceiling. In addition, a 148-foot Ferris wheel was built commemorating the world's first Ferris wheel that debuted at the World's Columbian Exhibition of 1893. The pier's Skyline Stage and 7-story Shakespeare Theater complement the IMAX theater and Crystal Gardens, which contain some seventy palm trees. A vast array of Chicago's finest restaurants have a home in here, as well as countless amusements, including a convention center with 170,000 square feet of exhibition space. North of the pier is the Milton Olive Park and the city's water filtration plant, the largest in America.

Chicago's oldest park, Washington Square, was donated to the city by Orasmus Bushnell in 1842 as the focal point of his residential development bordered by State, Chicago, Division, and LaSalle. At first the park was used for public demonstrations, such as the protest against the hike in liquor-license fees by Germans, who owned many of the city's beer gardens in 1855. By the late 1800s, however, Washington Square was a genteel city park with a central fountain, where elegant ladies promenaded with baby carriages.

After 1900, as many buildings in the neighborhood were converted into rooming houses, the square became "the outdoor forum of garrulous hobohemia" known as Bughouse Square. Every Sunday, crowds gathered in the park to hear radical soapbox speakers, a tradition that still continues thanks to events sponsored by the Newberry Library, located on the square. Accordingly, a raised concrete speakers' platform was built in 1985. Most of the original buildings, including Unity Church, still line the square.

The Newberry Library at 60 West Walton Street and Washington Square, circa 1905. The independent, public, noncirculating library was founded with a bequest from one of Chicago's most successful real-estate tycoons, Walter J. Newberry. Designed by Henry Ives Cobb, a great student of H. H. Richardson, it was one of the city's most remarkable Romanesque revival structures. The façade was inspired by the twelfth-century church of Saint Giles-du-Gard in Southern France. Cobb was a very young architect and had already made his mark in Chicago by designing Potter Palmer's Rhine-style castle along Lake Shore Drive in 1882 for the imperious maven of Chicago society Bertha Honore Palmer. In addition, he designed the Chicago Historical Society Building (1892) on North Dearborn, known today as the nightclub Excalibur, and the Chicago Varnish Company building on Kinzie Street, which now houses baseball legend Harry Caray's Restaurant.

Today the Newberry Library stands as one of the world's great centers of research in the humanities. It has more than twenty-one miles of books along its shelves. Famed Chicago architect Harry Wesse restored the late-nineteenth-century character of the interior in 1983 and built a 10-story addition on the northwest end of the building, providing additional storage space for its 1.5 million books, 5 million manuscripts, and 300,000 maps in a state-of-the-art, temperature-controlled environment. Exterior cleaning in the 1990s brought back the heavy stone blocks' original pink-tinged hue. The unique material is studded with natural mica chips that catch the rays of the sun and sparkle in a lustrous and shimmering spectacle. Today many readers at the Newberry are amateur genealogists utilizing the extensive materials in family history. Washington Square has also undergone an extensive restoration and reshaping.

Dearborn and Walton on Washington Square, late 1860s. With its matched Gothic towers, Unity Church was touted as the grandest of Chicago's Joliet limestone churches when it was completed in 1867. This view shows precisely how rural the Washington Square area was throughout much of the nineteenth century. Designed by Theodore Wadskier, the church was gutted in the Great Fire of 1871. The external stone survived mostly intact, except for the towers.

After the fire, Dankmar Adler supervised the rebuilding, installing raked seating for better acoustics. In 1900, the church was sold to the Freemasons, who leveled the floor and removed the altar, but have maintained the church's woodwork, stained glass, and upper floors ever since. The Scottish Rite Cathedral, as it is now known, is one building in a complex of several Masonic buildings, including the Romanesque-style Thompson House (1888) next door. Located just across the street from the Newberry Library, this property is now one of Chicago's most valuable. A great boom is under way in the neighborhood. With the demolishing of the nearby McCormick YMCA building, a new 22-story residential building by Booth Hansen Associates has been constructed at 30 West Oak Street, adding a stunning new piece of architecture to the community. The Masons are now developing some of the empty property they once used for parking. Construction is scheduled to begin soon on new high-rises along State Street to the east.

Left: View east from the Clark Street Bridge, circa 1893. The river was Chicago's industrial lifeblood, jam-packed with freight-hauling vessels and lined with docks, warehouses, and factories. Land traffic was often delayed while ships passed through open bridges. *Inset:* View from the Rush Street Bridge, circa 1860s, with a steam tug towing a sailboat upriver. In 1863, stampeding cattle caused the bridge to collapse; more than a hundred animals died.

Above: Skyscrapers have replaced the industrial structures lining the riverbanks. The bridges still delay traffic, and there are more of them—one for every major north-south thoroughfare except Rush (the bridge was never rebuilt). One difference between these photos is invisible. To improve water quality, the city created the "eighth wonder of the world," a new canal and grade change that actually reversed the flow of the river. When the channel opened in 1900 with the river now flowing out of the lake, it was an engineering triumph to rival the Panama Canal.

The Lake, Randolph, and Madison street bridges seen in the hazy early morning light in the 1860s. Commercial buildings and wharves lined all shores of the river, including the South Branch, which led to the I&M Canal (the link to the Mississippi River). Traffic was bad when bridges were raised. Noted one 1850s commentator, "A row of vehicles and impatience frequently accumulates that is quite terrific. I have seen a closely-packed column a quarter of a mile in length, every individual driver looking as if he thought he could have turned the bridge sixteen times, while he had been waiting . . ."

Today, Chicago boasts the greatest number of movable bridges, fifty-two in all. Almost all are trunnion bascule (or seesaw) bridges. They still open in synchronization—what one writer called the "Ballet of Bridges"—much to the annoyance of pedestrians and motorists. It is truly a sight to behold. Gone are the commercial sailing vessels and low-slung wharves; the downtown South Branch is lined with tall buildings. At left are the Morton Building (1961), the Civic Opera House (1929), and the Chicago Mercantile Exchange Center (1983).

Northwest corner of North Dearborn and West Ontario streets, 1896. The Chicago Historical Society was founded in 1857, but its original building went up in flames in the Great Fire of 1871. In 1892, the Society commissioned Henry Ives Cobb to design this fireproof Richardsonian Romanesque structure as their headquarters. One admiring critic called it a "pyramidal pile of brownstone," and the building quickly garnered the nickname "The Castle" when it opened in 1892.

When the Chicago Historical Society moved to its present digs on the edge of Lincoln Park in 1931, the Castle became home to everything from a Moose lodge to WPA offices, from the prestigious Institute of Design to recording studios for influential blues and rock-and-roll performers in the 1950s and '60s. Attorney F. Lee Bailey purchased the building in the 1960s, converting it to a nightclub. When the surrounding River North neighborhood underwent a renaissance in the 1980s, the structure became a gigantic, multilevel dance club known as Excalibur.

Northeast corner of North State and East Superior Streets, circa 1874. In the wake of the Great Fire of 1871, Chicagoans launched a number of ambitious construction and reconstruction projects. The Catholic diocese of Chicago commissioned ecclesiastical architect Patrick Keeley to design a replacement for a smaller Victorian building destroyed in the fire. Its dedication in 1874 drew a crowd of more than 5,000 and featured a parade of eighteen bands and a twenty-five-priest choir. In 1880, the diocese of Chicago was made an archdiocese.

Holy Name Cathedral is a cornerstone of the River North neighborhood, and the archdiocese remains one of the most powerful influences in Chicago, serving over 2.5 million Roman Catholics. After renovations in 1914, the building was made fifteen feet longer. Pope John Paul II celebrated mass here in 1979, and both Luciano Pavarotti and the Chicago Symphony Orchestra have performed here. During Chicago's Gangland heyday, Capone rival Dion O'Banion was shot point-blank outside a neighboring flower shop; several bullets glanced off the cathedral.

North Branch of the Chicago River, circa 1909. As early as the 1830s, the North Branch became the focus of manufacturing activity when the city's first meat-packing plant was established there. A lumber mill soon followed (note the Schillo Lumber Company seen here), and the North Branch became the most heavily industrial section of the river. Goose Island was created in the 1860s when the North Branch canal was dug on its north side. Goose Island was once known as Kilgubbin, when it was the home of a rough brand of Irish "faction fighters" who would brain you as soon as look at you. The island received its nickname from Chicago mayor Long John Wentworth, the 6'6" former congressman who remarked on all the geese kept there.

By 1924, Goose Island was home to meat-processing, chemical, electrical, and food and brewing enterprises. With the decline of hard industry in the United States, Goose Island also suffered, but today it has been reinvigorated thanks to government tax incentives. In the last ten years, Federal Express, Republic Windows, and Sara Lee have moved their facilities to Goose Island, and the beer-making history lives on in Chicago's Goose Island Brewery. Today the southeastern tip of the island in the North Branch is home to Kendall College, 900 N. North Branch Street. Their School of Culinary Arts has made this a secret destination for refined diners who appreciate the cuisine presented by student chefs and future restaurateurs.

Northwest corner of Adams and Desplaines, circa 1880s. Constructed between 1852 and 1856, St. Patrick's Roman Catholic Church was designed by Carter & Bauer of Milwaukee common (yellow) brick above a Joliet limestone base. The onion dome at right was meant to symbolize the Church in the East, the spire, the Church in the West.

Saved from the path of the Chicago Fire, Old St. Patrick Church remains Chicago's oldest continuous use building and thriving Catholic urban parish. At the turn of the century, Chicago artist Thomas A. O'Shaughnessy, whose father supervised the construction of the I&M Canal, designed the rare stained-glass windows encrusted in Irish motifs and festooned the interior with complex designs from the ancient *Book of Kells*. Later, when the neighborhood became heavily industrialized and residents abandoned it, the church fell on hard times. In the 1940s, the pastor even painted over the Celtic designs with thick, pink paint. Its rich splendor sat hidden until a 1990s renovation project transformed the worship space and restored the elegance of O'Shaughnessy's designs. Old St. Pat's, as it is affectionately known, remains the heart of Chicago's Irish Catholic community. The summer block party here goes on for three days and nights and draws young people from across Chicagoland.

West Randolph at Desplaines, 1892. Where Randolph Street widens as it approaches Halsted Street was the center of wholesale produce distribution. On May 4, 1886, a bomb went off at a workers' rally in this Haymarket district, killing one policeman instantly. Officers opened fire on the crowd, killing as many as ten and wounding more than thirty. A total of eight policemen died, many injured by police fire. In what was later deemed very dubious justice, eight anarchists were sentenced to death. Four were hanged, one committed suicide, and three were later pardoned.

The statue at lower right of the archival photo is a police officer with an upraised arm, restraining an invisible mob. The plaque commands peace "In the name of the people of Illinois." The controversy surrounding the riot plagued the statue as well, which was repeatedly vandalized; in 1903, for example, a streetcar motorman intentionally rammed it. The statue was moved to Union Park, where it was again defaced during the civil unrest of the 1960s. It resides today at the

Police Training Academy. The legacy of the anarchists has dwindled in a city that prides itself on its robust role in the American labor movement. Once thick with the storefronts of wholesale grocers, Randolph Street is now restaurant row, with chic high-end restaurants and clubs. Even the old headquarters of the Catholic Charities has come down, soon to be replaced by new condos that will reconfigure the neighborhood.

800 South Halsted at Polk Street, circa 1912. Built in 1856 for wealthy real-estate baron Charles J. Hull, this brick Italianate house was originally in a chic neighborhood, but the elite moved north to follow Potter Palmer, and the West Side became the "port of entry" for many of Chicago's immigrant groups. In 1889, Jane Addams and her college friend moved into this house to live among and help Chicago's poor immigrant communities. By the turn of the century, the settlement complex consisted of thirteen buildings covering a city block.

In 1931, Jane Addams became the first American woman to win the Nobel Peace Prize; she was acknowledged for her work for a variety of good causes: women's suffrage, child-labor laws, and better schools and sanitation, among others. In the 1960s, this site became part of a large parcel of land slated for development by the city into the new University of Illinois at Chicago. In 1963, the university dedicated the original Charles Hull home as a museum of the settlement but tore down all the other buildings in the complex.

Chicago is a town of immigrant communities, particularly the West Side. When Jane Addams established Hull House in this neighborhood, she described the ethnic patchwork: "Between Halsted Street and the river live about 10,000 Italians. In the south on 12th Street are many Germans, and side streets are given over to Polish and Russian Jews. Still farther south, thin Jewish colonies merge into a huge Bohemian colony." To the northwest were French Canadians, Irish to the north, and beyond them, other "well-to-do English speaking families." Once families achieved a modicum of success, they often moved on to better-off immigrant communities, leaving their "ghettos" for incoming immigrant groups.

In the archival photo is Anshe Sholom Synagogue at 733 South Ashland at Polk Street. Built shortly after the turn of the century, the building was sold when the congregation moved out west to what was then called "Chicago's Jerusalem" in Douglas Park. Today, Anshe Sholom B'nai Chicago is on the city's North Side. The original Greek Revival–style building, designed by Alexander Levy, was converted to a Greek Orthodox church in 1927. Today, St. Basil's is almost seventy-five years old. Located on the University of Illinois campus, the building's ribbed dome is now covered with shingles, but the original Hebrew carving is still visible on the portico.

558 West DeKoven Street, 1871. It had been a hot, dry summer, and the whole Midwest was suffering a tremendous drought. Chicago, with its preponderance of wooden balloon-frame buildings, wooden sidewalks, and wooden tar-sealed paving blocks, was a tinderbox in search of a spark. On a windy Sunday evening, October 8, 1871, a fire broke out in the barn behind Patrick and Catherine O'Leary's West Side home. Within hours, a raging inferno had jumped the river twice and laid waste to the downtown. "Fire devils," whirling pockets of gas and air, rolled through the city streets for two days afterward, flattening buildings and sending survivors running into the lake. Eyewitness accounts relate that the heat of the fire was so intense the sand beaches melted into rough glass.

Three hundred Chicagoans died, 90,000 were made homeless, 17,500 buildings were destroyed, and total damages amounted to $200 million. Nevertheless, the Fire became the defining moment in Chicago's history, igniting the fierce spark of can-do pride and civic boosterism that led the *Chicago Tribune* to print in its first post-Fire edition (October 11): "CHEER UP! In the midst of a calamity without parallel in the world's history, looking upon the ashes of 30 years' accumulations, the people of this once beautiful city have resolved that CHICAGO SHALL RISE AGAIN!" Within two years, the city was essentially completely rebuilt. Today, on the site of the fire's origin stands the Chicago Fire Academy with its red-glazed brick exterior. A flame-shaped sculpture by Egon Weiner commemorates the Fire.

St. Ignatius College was founded in 1869 as a Jesuit Institution. It is the city's oldest school and one of the only Chicago examples of decidedly French architecture, a rare and distinctive example of institutional design predating the Chicago Fire of 1871. Designed by Toussaint Menard, the building contains typical features of a nineteenth-century school, such as the top-floor assembly room, where it was structurally easier to include clear span space. In 1873, the fourth floor housed a natural history museum.

Loyola University originated from this institution but, since 1922, St. Ignatius has operated solely as a college preparatory school. It now sits on the edge of the University of Illinois campus on Chicago's West Side (1076 West Roosevelt). The streetcars are gone and the road is now paved, but the German Gothic–style Holy Family Church (1860) still stands, a testament to the German craftsmen of this neighborhood. The statue is of the school's pioneering founder, Father Arnold Damen, SJ.

1633 North Cleveland, 1871. In 1852, Chicago's German community built a small church in the center of their North Side neighborhood, then known as "North Town." They replaced it with a much grander redbrick building with a two-hundred-foot spire in 1869, only to see it gutted by the Great Fire of 1871. The picturesque remains seen here were declared the "most impressive remains on the North Side."

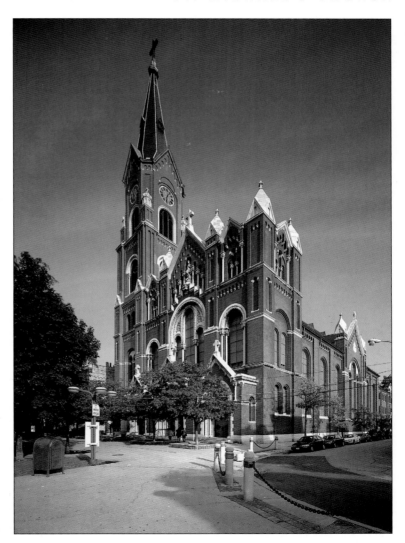

Today, St. Michael's is the heart and soul of the Old Town neighborhood, whose very boundaries are determined by their relationship to the church: if you can hear St. Michael's bells tolling, you are in Old Town. After the Great Fire, determined parishioners rebuilt in just one year; the steeple and clock were added in 1888 and the Munich stained-glass windows in 1902. The neighborhood is gentrified today.

In the midst of an extremely hot Chicago-style summer, during which several people died from the heat, many Chicagoans opted to go to the movies; theaters had recently been advertising that they were "air cooled." The Biograph, at 2433 North Lincoln, was one such "refrigerated" theater, and on July 22, 1934, one of Chicago's most famous gangsters, wanted for multiple bank robbery and murder, met his fate there.

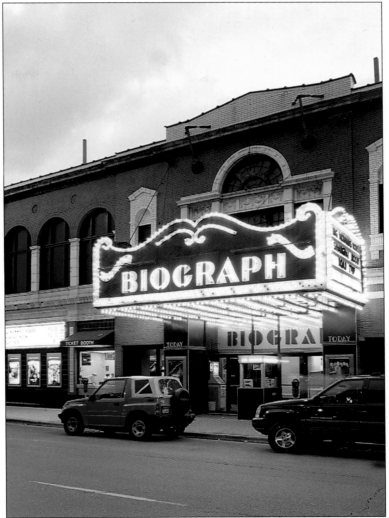

On his birthday a month earlier, John Dillinger had been declared "Public Enemy Number One" by the FBI. When he exited the show that evening, twenty lawmen were waiting. Betrayed by the "Lady in Red," his girlfriend's landlady, Dillinger was gunned down as he tried to flee. Today, the ethos of the Dillinger shooting still captures the attention of Chicagoans and visitors alike. For decades, when the Biograph was still a movie theater, Manhattan Melodrama, the movie showing on the night of Dillinger's shooting, was often replayed. The power of Public Enemy Number One still pervades the narrow alley next door, where the Lady in Red is said to have lured him to federal agents. In 2006, the Biograph was reborn (above) as a new theater for stage productions of the Victory Garden theater company, one of Chicago's premier production companies. Its renovation ushered in a new generation of theatrical use, though the strange historic past of the building will be hard to shake. As a Chicago landmark its value is without measure.

Like the rest of the North Side, this area was considered inaccessible and remote for most of the nineteenth century—remote enough that the lakefront beyond North Avenue was used as the city cemetery. In 1864, the city agreed to move the cemetery farther north ("In Chicago, even the dead must 'move on,' " remarked one commentator), and dedicated Lake Park. It was renamed Lincoln Park the following year in honor of the assassinated president.

Today, Lincoln Park, at 5.5 miles, is the city's largest park. The park contains the free Lincoln Park Zoo; monuments to Lincoln, Grant, and Hamilton; a conservatory; the Nature Museum; the Chicago Historical Society; a community theater; a city beach and bathhouse; two ponds, and a lagoon large enough to accommodate rowing and sculling practice. The surrounding area is also called Lincoln Park and is today one of the city's most desirable—and expensive—neighborhoods.

Already one of the busier intersections in turn-of-the-century Lincoln Park, Halsted, Fullerton, and Lincoln were home to a high-class residential district throughout the 1930s. Formerly German farmland, the neighborhood has an ethnic heritage that is reflected in the shop names. After World War II, however, many homes were converted into tenement rooming houses, and by the 1950s, the rise of the suburbs meant the blighting of Lincoln Park.

No neighborhood in Chicago has undergone more refined or redefining restoration than Lincoln Park. The leafy neighborhood enjoys some of the city's highest real-estate price tags. Between the lakefront and Halsted Street, this mile-wide environ is lush with elegance and character. On the western end here at Lincoln Avenue, Fullerton Street, and Halsted Street, Children's Memorial Hospital is ranked as one of the largest landowners. But new plans call for the world-class children's facility to move downtown to the medical campus of Northwestern University. Also nearby, DePaul University's Lincoln Park Campus has exploded into what has been called "America's happiest university campus." The community retains an old Chicago charm, honeycombed with an endless array of saloons and groggeries in one of the city's hippest neighborhoods.

Chicago's most iconic 1920s Prohibition-era gangland slayings took place here in a truck garage at 2122 N. Clark Street on Valentine's Day in 1929. The event seized the attention of the nation. The bloodbath pitted the forces of Al Capone, the city's undisputed crime boss, against his Irish rival George "Bugs" Moran for control of the city's vast bootlegging empire. Capone's henchmen, disguised as Chicago police, caught the Moran gang off-guard on a cold, snowy winter morning. Seven of Moran's men were executed. The St. Valentine's Day Massacre was immortalized by Hollywood and remains a frozen moment of Chicago's "Roaring Twenties" past.

All physical reminders of the SMC Cartage Company garage have long since been wiped away by more sensitive generations of Chicagoans, especially the late mayor Richard J. Daley, who had little patience for the city's Prohibition relics. The garage was torn down in 1967. Thus passed the city's most singular shrine to the 1920s bootlegging mayhem. The small grassy lawn of what today is a senior citizen residence is all that remains of that haunted parcel of Chicago real estate. There are, however, many residents and neighbors who, with a long list of eerie sounds and sightings, claim the ghosts of the past still remain.

Like many of Chicago's diagonal roads, Milwaukee began life as a Native American trail that became a plank road and a streetcar route, and helped populate the northwest side with more recent immigrants. The intersection seen here is the commercial heart of a Polish neighborhood that became known as Wicker Park after the triangular-shaped public park that developer-politician Charles Wicker and his brother Joel donated to the city in 1870.

After a long slide into blight after the Polish community moved farther out, Wicker Park is undergoing a renaissance. The Blue Line el follows the northwest curve of Milwaukee Avenue, enabling residents and visitors to make the short nine-minute subway ride in record time to the Damen Avenue Station. Hot clubs, edgy coffeehouses, intriguing bookstores, and a seemingly endless array of top restaurants have recently helped the neighborhood attain a cult status: Chicago's own version of New York's Greenwich Village. Nearby streets are lined with some of the city's largest and best examples of Victorian-era architecture, earning the area the nickname the "Polish Gold Coast."

One of America's first Polish churches, St. Stanislaus was founded in 1868. Wealthy Polish beer magnates helped fund the commission of architect Patrick Keeley, who had just finished the Holy Name Cathedral downtown, to design a church in honor of the St. Stanislaus Kostka, SJ, who was named for the patron saint of Poland. The building was constructed between 1876 and 1881 in brick. The towers were added in 1892 under direction of German architect Adolphus Druiding, and this photo was taken around that time.

The grandeur of St. Stanislaus Kostka shimmers with renewed vitality and a freshly restored architectural character. Once the gateway for new Polish immigrants in the nineteenth century, today it is the center of a vast urban rebirth. A new population of young urban professionals is discovering the desirability of this community only two miles from downtown. When Chicago was constructing the Northwest Expressway in 1960, St. Stanislaus Kostka Church escaped destruction when Mayor Richard J. Daley permitted the highway to curve around the building. Today speedy motorists get a jolt when they fly past the windows of the parish rectory, just inches from the fast lane. Nearby Rostenkowski Park recalls the generations of powerful Polish politicos who ruled this area of the city, not least of which was former Congressman Dan Rostenkowski, the longtime chairman of the House Ways and Means Committee.

The once heavily Russian neighborhood known as "Ukrainian Village" brings together two powerful architectural traditions. Here, in this 1903 photo, Chicago's signature architect Louis Sullivan, father of the great Chicago School, blended these potent artistic forms and created Holy Trinity Russian Orthodox Cathedral at 1121 N. Leavitt Street, in a neighborhood of onion-domed churches. Modeled on the great St. Vladimir's Cathedral in Kiev, this compact structure is a stunning exposition of the Prairie style. Its stucco plastering of exterior walls and measured scale—replete with Sullivan's trademark decorative metalwork—is a rich and unexpected expression of the style that Sullivan's pupil Frank Lloyd Wright would later make famous. Tsar Nicholas II, the last of the Romanovs, partially paid for this liturgical outpost of Russian faith and culture.

A century later, this exotic cathedral flexes the artistry of its design even more powerfully, emboldened by a dome of fresh gold leaf. Now enjoying the benefits of a neighborhood with a renewed economic vitality, Holy Trinity Cathedral still echoes with the haunting chants of its ancient liturgical traditions. The interior is a powerful expression of timeless faith, with encrusted icons that cover the doorway to heaven.

Since the canonization of the Romanov martyrs who perished at the hands of the Bolshevik fanatics of the Russian Revolution more than eighty years ago, today the royal faces of the imperial family enjoy a fresh sanctity in a shrine dedicated to their honor. Clouds of incense continue to rise to the glory of God in prayer amid the artistry of Chicago's most remarkable architect.

West on Addison, circa 1915. One of the oldest ballparks in the country (certainly the oldest in the National League), Wrigley Field was built in 1914 and designed by Zachary Taylor Davis, who also designed the first Comiskey Park. A live bear cub was on hand when the team played its first game. Originally called Weeghman Park after the first owner, the park was renamed when William Wrigley purchased the team in 1926. Dedicated to tradition, for years Wrigley was one of the only major-league stadiums to change numbers by hand and to forego modern lighting.

Within the "Friendly Confines" of Wrigley Field, baseball history has often shaped the contours of this last great American ballpark. Here, during the 1932 World Series, Babe Ruth hit his famous "called shot" to the bleachers for a home run that just might be the most memorable in baseball. The Chicago Cubs, in 1988, were the last team in baseball to begin hosting night games, "under the glare of the electric lights." This is an old-fashioned park where 39,000 fans show up to watch their beloved team. In the surrounding neighborhood known as "Wrigleyville," the population is bright and successful—and relentless about the Cubs. It has often been said that the Chicago White Sox are a "Southside team," but the Cubs are a Chicago team. The Cubs have not played in a World Series since 1945 and have not won a World Series since 1908.

South from Byron Street, abutting Graceland Cemetery, 1905. One of the last real-estate developments of Samuel Eberly Gross, a colorful investor responsible for the development of thousands of working-class Chicago homes, Alta Vista Terrace is sometimes called the "Street of Forty Doors." The ensemble of forty row houses was designed by J. C. Brompton between 1900 and 1904 and modeled on moderately priced Georgian row houses Gross had just seen in London.

Alta Vista Terrace was designated Chicago's first historic district in 1971, setting standards for maintenance and preservation. The lively, human-sized terrace was designed as a street-long unit, but with an abundance of personalized contrasts in color, roofline, and architectural detail. The individual house designs are mirrored diagonally, so the southernmost home on the east side is the same as the northernmost on the west, and so on.

1345 West Argyle Street, Uptown, 1910s. For ten years (1907–1917), a pioneering movie studio turned Chicago into "Hollywood on the prairie." Essanay Studios (an amalgam of the founders' initials—S and A) boasted silent cinema's greatest stars on its contract roster: Charlie Chaplin, Gloria Swanson, Francis X. Bushman, and "Bronco Billy" Anderson (a cofounder). The studio dominated the market in westerns and comedies. *Inset*: A promotional piece for a film shot in Chicago. Gloria Swanson is third from the left.

Changes in the movie industry (a shift to the clement climes of California—most movies were shot outdoors), the defection of Charlie Chaplin to a competitor, and internal dissension led to Essanay's collapse. Today, the building houses St. Augustine's College, a small liberal arts school. The terra-cotta Indian heads flanking the entrance were Essanay's trademarks. Argyle Street, once relatively rural, is today the heart of Little Saigon, Chicago's Vietnamese neighborhood.

850 West Exchange Avenue at Peoria. Designed by preeminent city architects Burnham & Root in 1879, the Union Stock Yard Gate gave a majestic face to a sprawling 475-plus-acre Union Stock Yard (est. 1865), when Chicago was "hog butcher to the world," using every part of the pig "but the squeal." Tourist guidebooks of the mid-nineteenth century marveled at the scale and efficiency of the operation. Writers had already branded Chicago "The Great Bovine City of the World," thanks to the major role Chicago played in supplying Union troops with beef during the Civil War. *Inset:* Almost a city in itself, the yards included pen space for up to 25,000 cattle, 80,000 hogs, and 25,000 sheep.

The publication of Upton Sinclair's *The Jungle* in 1906 led to reforms in sanitation and labor conditions for the yards, but Chicago still dominated the meat-packing industry. After providing employment for the Bridgeport and Back of the Yards communities for over a century, the Union Stock Yard closed in 1971. The gate was designated a Chicago Landmark in 1972. The "bust" over the central limestone arch is thought to be "Sherman," a prize-winning steer named after the yard's cofounder, John B. Sherman. Today, industrial parks have filled in some of the vacant space where slaughterhouses once stood.

Shields and 35th, 1913. Built in 1910 and designed by Zachary Taylor Davis, who would go on to design Wrigley Field as well, the original Comiskey billed itself in typical Chicago hyperbole as "Baseball Palace to the World." Home to the American League's White Sox, Comiskey also was the venue for a variety of events, including several boxing title fights, Beatles concerts, and, evidently, "auto polo."

After the owner threatened to move the White Sox franchise, the city sought state financing to build a new facility on an adjacent lot. On September 30, 1990, the last game was played at the original Comiskey Park, and the following year, America's oldest ballpark was torn down.

A plaque in the giant parking lot marks old home plate, and the park is now renamed U.S. Cellular Field. The White Sox won the American League Pennant in 2005 and went on to triumph in the World Series, their first such win since 1917.

View west on 18th Street at Racine, circa 1908. The lower West Side boomed after the Great Fire of 1871, when burned-out industries and workers moved west. Immigrants from Bohemia were the earliest settlers, and they named the neighborhood after the second largest Czech city. At center, St. Procopius, built in 1883 and designed by Julius Huber, honors Bohemia's patron saint.

Today, the Romanesque Revival–style St. Procopius is considered the "mother church" of Chicago's many Bohemian parishes. However, in the tradition of churches serving immigrant neighborhoods, it has kept pace with the community. By the late 1900s, Pilsen, and next-door Little Village, were steadily becoming Chicago's biggest Mexican neighborhoods. Eighteenth Street is now the central thoroughfare of one of the city's most dynamic Hispanic neighborhoods. Authentic Mexican eateries are plentiful, and the diversity of the population is a remarkable mix of Mexican immigrants, yuppies, and hipsters.

Chicago's original Chinatown began in the 1870s with the arrival of Chinese workers on the vast system of railroads that all led to Chicago. The Midwest provided a more welcoming environment than the prohibitive sanctions meted out to Chinese people in the Western states. Settlement for Chinese in Chicago began around Clark and Van Buren Streets in the saloon-and-brothel-ridden First Ward, known as the Levee District. Vice gradually gave way to more legitimate business

ventures downtown. The Chinese community moved farther south along Wentworth Avenue and 22nd Street. Modern Chinatown traces its origins to 1912, when a large group of Chinese immigrants was displaced from the South Loop by a construction project. The Chinese Benevolent Association (On Leong) negotiated fifty leases for shops and flats en masse, and Chinatown was born almost overnight.

After the revolution of Mao in China in the late 1940s, Chinese immigration to Chicago multiplied. A huge surge in population increased the density of the neighborhood, with Chinese immigrants taking over a section of the community once the reserve of Italian and Croation immigrants in North Bridgeport. Two powerful urban development projects in the late 1950s and 1960s—the construction of the Dan Ryan Expressway and the building of the Red Line elevated line—changed the contours of Chinatown. Today Chinatown flourishes more than ever. An expansion of commercial enterprise in the 1990s built a vast new center of shops, restaurants, and residential buildings. Chinatown's colorful lacquered gate is a symbol of the area's vibrancy and cultural enrichment. New immigrants, especially from Hong Kong, have brightened the commercial climate of this thriving neighborhood.

57th and Greenwood, circa 1905. The first University of Chicago, which opened in 1857, went bankrupt in 1886. It wasn't until the 1890s, when John D. Rockefeller pledged $35 million to create a university to rival "Princeton and Yale," and department store magnate Marshall Field donated the land, that the U of C took shape. Architect Henry Ives Cobb designed the campus as a self-contained Gothic village. Culver Hall is at left; the Anatomy Building at right, both designed by Cobb in 1897. The Olmsted Brothers designed Hull Courtyard and the gate in 1903.

Most universities gradually achieve renown over time; the University of Chicago seemed to spring fully formed from the collaboration of its great early leaders. Today, the school has over 10,000 students attending prestigious graduate programs in law, medicine, business, and theology (among others). The university claims sixty-seven Nobel Prize winners (between students and faculty), more than any other university. Since the Nobel Prize in economics was instituted in 1969, the U of C has had a virtual monopoly on the award: seventeen wins, which averages out to one every other year.

Chicago's Hyde Park–Kenwood community boasts six important Frank Lloyd Wright–designed domestic residences, all from the early period of his success. But no home is more internationally acclaimed than the Robie House, built in 1909. Bicycle manufacturer Frederick C. Robie, like most of Wright's clients, was a self-made man of intelligence and modernity. He wanted to be free of the clutter and "conglomeration" to which architecture had become tied. He had a specific list of architectural demands that others found too edgy for the times. Not so Frank Lloyd Wright. Most critically, Robie longed for rooms without interruption and windows without curvature. He wanted all the daylight he could get to fill his house and the ability to look out from his house without compromising his own privacy to the staring eyes of others. With Wright, he would achieve all this and more—a true classic of modern architecture.

The Robie House is considered the best of example of the Prairie School of architecture. It remains dramatic, with the most expansive of Wright's horizontal proportions. Wright achieved this by his total use of narrow Roman brick that he had specially made in St. Louis. The backbone of the house was formed of fifteen-inch channel beams more than a hundred feet long, fabricated in Chicago by Ryerson Steel. In addition to the sweeping cantilevering, Wright experimented with indirect lighting around the side walls of the living room. Indirect heating, which Wright would use throughout his career with mixed results, was first introduced at the Robie House. Robie relished the prospect of his feet never having to hit a cold floor, so radiators were actually contained in the floors and heat rose from beneath. Today the Robie House is owned the University of Chicago. In 1997, the Frank Lloyd Wright Preservation Trust assumed management, restoration, and interpretation of the house.

Built on reclaimed swampland at the edge of the lakefront's Jackson Park, the "composite" building materials employed for the fair—a mixture of hemp and plaster—gave all its structures only a temporary life. However, after the fair's conclusion and the subsequent fire that destroyed most of the remaining buildings, this majestic structure was made more permanent and became the first home of the Field Museum until 1921. At that time, Julius Rosenwald, the president of Sears, Roebuck & Co., endowed a new museum to be like the Deutches Museum in Munich, providing funds to establish interactive exhibitions. A $5 million renovation transformed the building into a more permanent Museum of Industry. In 1928, the name officially changed to the Museum of Science and Industry. Opening in 1933, it was ready for the second great Chicago World's Fair, the Century of Progress, celebrating the city's centennial.

After World War II, the Museum of Science and Industry became one of Chicago's most venerated attractions. Nothing captured people's attention more than the U-505, the German submarine captured on the high seas during the war. The man responsible for the capture, Captain (later Admiral) Daniel Gallery, was a Chicago native. He helped local business leaders acquire the U-boat from the U.S. Navy and have it brought through the St. Lawrence Seaway and all the

Great Lakes to its new home. Once there, the submarine was lifted from the water and moved to a permanent home. Fifty years later, in 2005, the vessel was moved to a special controlled exhibition site that protects this reminder of the last great conflict. The museum today counts more than 350,000 square feet of space in which more than 800 exhibition and 2,000 interactive sites welcome more than 2 million visitors each year.

Although Hyde Park would not become an official part of Chicago until 1889, the area was developed as an exclusive residential neighborhood with easy access to downtown via the train. To further suburban beautification, the South Park Commission hired Frederick Law Olmsted, designer of New York's Central Park, to design an extensive system of connected parks and landscaped boulevards on the South Side. Until the middle of the twentieth century, Chicagoans would train or ferry down for a day in the park.

Part of Jackson Park, which in turn is part of the Olmsted-designed South Park system, 57th Street Beach was a swamp that had to be dredged in the 1870s and then paved with granite blocks in the 1880s in time for the 1893 World's Fair. Today, the waterfront from 56th down to 63rd street is utilized mostly by local Hyde Parkers in the summer. Lake Shore Drive, today almost a full-blown highway, has replaced the earlier forest and made access to the beaches more difficult.

West side of Hyde Park. Washington Park was designed by Frederick Law Olmsted in 1871 as the "Upper Division" of great South Park, connected to the "Lower Division," or Jackson Park, by the narrow Midway Plaisance. If Jackson Park was a swamp, Washington was a prairie flatland not naturally well suited to a manicured public park. It was also the endpoint of three traffic-filled boulevards—Garfield, Drexel, and Grand (now MLK).

Olmsted's final plan combined the best of nature and design—the northern end, 100 acres in all, comprises a "large meadowy ground"; the southern half sports a manmade lagoon with verdant landscaping. The archival photo was taken in 1889, during the heyday of the Victorian penchant for floral design. Save floral design, many of the same activities—picnicking, biking, socializing with family—are enjoyed in the park today.

Rather than building a factory in the city amid the workers, railroad sleeping car magnate George Pullman decided to build a city around his factory. The first model industrial (planned) community in the United States, Pullman, on the city's far South Side, was designed in the 1880s by renowned Chicago architect Solon Beman. The town included everything the worker might need—a school, library, theater, church, bank, post office, and so on. Taverns, however, were banned. Pullman's workers (all 20,000) were required to live in the tidy little brick row houses, with expensive modern conveniences (such as indoor plumbing and gas) provided at reasonable rents—and an annual 6 percent profit for Pullman.

Business plummeted in the depression of 1893, so Pullman fired thousands of workers and sliced wages 25 percent for those remaining. However, he refused to lower rents, resulting in near-starvation conditions. The workers went on strike, and in spring of 1894, the American Railway Union led by Eugene V. Debs voted to support the Pullman strike. After a few episodes of violence, President Cleveland sent in federal troops. Pullman died in 1897, and the town was sold to its residents in 1907. The entire district was declared a National Historic Landmark in 1971, but its isolated position ten miles from downtown has made a complete renaissance difficult.

951 Chicago Avenue, Oak Park. Seen here somewhat overgrown in 1926 after being divided up into multiple apartments is the original Frank Lloyd Wright home and studio. Wright's great passion was residential design; during his career he created over 270 homes, but this was his first. Wright used the home as a laboratory, constantly revising, rebuilding, and adding on. Some kernels of his later theories can be seen here in the stark geometric shapes, horizontal banding, and organic, flowing interior. Wright lived and worked here between 1889 and 1909 with his first wife, Catherine, and their six children.

Today, the home is a National Historic Landmark and museum. The FLW Home and Studio Foundation has restored it to appear as it did in 1909. The interior is also fully restored and features Art Deco wall paintings and a chain-supported balcony in the architecture studio.

Technically a suburb of Chicago, Oak Park boasts the world's largest collection of Wright-designed buildings. Wright lived in the streetcar suburb until 1909, when he fled to Europe with his lover, Mamah Borthwick Cheney.

INDEX